The Christmas Tree
GOD'S MESSAGE HIDDEN IN ITS BRANCHES

WIPF & STOCK · Eugene, Oregon

Mathew Bartlett

Wipf and Stock Publishers
199 W 8th Ave, Suite 3
Eugene, OR 97401

The Christmas Tree
God's Message Hidden in it's Branches
By Bartlett, Mathew
Copyright©2017 Apostolos
ISBN 13: 978-1-5326-6879-1
Publication date 9/15/2018
Previously published by Apostolos, 2017

Contents

Introduction

Since its mysterious introduction in 17th century Germany (some legends date it as far back as Martin Luther in 1500), and its subsequent arrival in Britain in the 19th century, at the request of Prince Albert, the Christmas tree has taken a permanent place in the hearts of people all over the world.

Generally, each year as the advent season approaches, an evergreen spruce or fir tree is cut and placed in homes, stores, and public spaces; although plastic trees are increasingly popular in many homes, since they last longer and leave no sharp fir needles on the floor! Once in place, the trees are lavishly decorated with baubles, tinsel, gifts and other decorations.

Have you ever wondered why Christians celebrate Christmas by putting up and decorating Christmas trees in this way? What on earth has a Christmas tree got to do with the birth of Jesus Christ anyway?

Your Christmas tree is full of meaning, every decoration tells its own unique story. Each bauble and light is filled with spiritual significance revealing something of God's message of love to the world.

In the flowing pages, we will take a look at the tree, with its familiar decorations, and examine what these represent to us in relation to the Christmas story.

Beautiful Decorations

Why do you make your home beautiful for Christmas—what could possibly be the meaning behind all that effort?

When we decorate our homes for the Christmas season, we are expressing our joy that Jesus has come into the world. It is also a symbol of the joy which shall be in heaven, a beauty that was brought into clear focus when Jesus left heaven's glory for the cold and dirt of the stable in Bethlehem.

Heaven is such a beautiful place, that it doesn't need to be decorated with baubles, tinsel, or lights, such as those we put on our Christmas trees. Yet someone who was once given a vision of heaven, the apostle John, said that it was beautifully decorated, with a foundation of precious stones, gates made of pearls, and streets which looked like pure transparent gold. No doubt this description is symbolic, for heaven is beautiful beyond description.

> *The foundations of the city's wall are decorated with every kind of precious stone. The first foundation is jasper, the second sapphire, the third agate, the fourth emerald, the fifth onyx, the sixth carnelian, the seventh chrysolite, the eighth beryl, the ninth topaz, the tenth chrysoprase, the eleventh jacinth, and the twelfth amethyst. And the twelve gates are twelve pearls -- each one of the gates is made from just one pearl! The main street of the city is pure gold, like transparent glass. (Rev 21:19–21)*

Such adornment makes our meagre Christmas decorations seem rather cheap, and yet it is true that every decoration on our Christmas tree is filled with a symbolic meaning which describes heavenly realities.

The wonder of Christmas is that people, although imperfect, will someday share the glory and reality of heaven—because of the child who was born in a stable!

The Tree

When I put up a Christmas tree in my home, surrounded by gift boxes, it reminds me of the greatest gift of all that hung from a tree—the Son of God who died for you and me.

Of course, the tree on which Jesus was crucified was neither decorated nor beautiful. It was cruel and ugly; the meanest thing humanity could devise in its war against God. However, the cross of Jesus carries a beauty all its own. It was on the cross that Jesus suffered and died, as the greatest expression of God's love for all people. The death of Jesus was carefully planned and foretold by God to be the means of our salvation.

> *"He himself bore our sins" in his body on the cross, so that we might die to sins and live for righteousness; "by his wounds you have been healed." (2 Peter 2:24)*

Many churches are decorated with crosses all year round, to remind Christians of the awful cost which Jesus paid to bring about our salvation; but at Christmas, we choose a very different—and far more attractive—symbol. At Christmas, we choose to put up an evergreen tree, evergreen meaning that their leaves do not die in the autumn. For although Jesus died on the cross, he rose again, and now lives forever.

The reason Jesus was born at Christmas was to save humanity from the finality of death. Since Jesus rose from the dead, the life which he offers to all who believe in him will last forever; it is a quality of life which only Jesus can give us—eternal life.

In the apostle John's vision of heaven, eternal life was symbolised by a tree called 'the tree of life':

> *Then the angel showed me the river of the water of life -- water as clear as crystal -- pouring out from the throne of God and of the Lamb, flowing down the middle of the city's main street. On each*

side of the river is the tree of life producing twelve kinds of fruit, yielding its fruit every month of the year. Its leaves are for the healing of the nations. (Rev 22:1–2)

In this picture, the tree of life, beside the river of the water of life, takes the central place in heaven. Of course, both symbols speak of Jesus, the centre of attraction in heaven.

As I write, I have yet to decide where to place my tree when I put it up in the living room. It might go in the corner, or in front of the window, or sometimes it goes on the table beside the phone. I'm sure I wouldn't be able to put it in the centre of the room!

Yet throughout this advent season, it is my heartfelt desire to put Jesus at the centre of all my celebrations, all my family gatherings, and of every area of my life. Perhaps you share my desire too? Let's put Jesus in the centre of our lives this Christmas!

The Angel

Near the top of my tree, I always put an angel.

Angels are God's special messengers, bringing good news for all the world. It was an angel who first told Mary and Joseph of the coming of a Saviour, and it was angels who informed the shepherds that a Saviour had been born for all people—Christ the Lord.

Frequently, the Bible describes the angels *singing*. Have you ever wondered what angels sing about?

The Angels Sing of a Saviour in a Manger

The first news of the birth of Jesus was not given to kings, or sent to Mary's relatives, nor even made known in the 'births' column of the local press! Angels brought the news to humble shepherds, telling them:

> *Do not be afraid. I bring you good news that will cause great joy for all the people. Today in the town of David a Savior has been born to you; he is the Messiah, the Lord. This will be a sign to you: You will find a baby wrapped in cloths and lying in a manger. (Luke 2:10–12)*

The Angels Sing of a Saviour in the Heart

Jesus said that whenever a person repents (turns back to God), and invites him in to share their lives (hearts), the angels in heaven rejoice and sing for joy:

> *I tell you that in the same way there will be more rejoicing in heaven over one sinner who repents than over ninety-nine righteous persons who do not need to repent. (Luke 15:7)*

The Angels Sing of a Saviour on the Throne

The Bible tells us that in heaven there will be a vast number of angels praising God for all that he has done for humankind by sending his only son to be the Saviour of the world.

> Then I looked and heard the voice of many angels in a circle around the throne, as well as the living creatures and the elders. Their number was ten thousand times ten thousand -- thousands times thousands --all of whom were singing in a loud voice: "Worthy is the lamb who was killed to receive power and wealth and wisdom and might and honor and glory and praise!" (Rev 5:11–12)

The angels still praise God every day and every night for sending Jesus to our world; and the angel on our Christmas tree reminds us to join with them in praising God this Christmas!

The Star

At the very top of my Christmas tree I place a star, to remind me of the star which led the wise men from the east to Jesus.

> *After Jesus was born in Bethlehem in Judea, during the time of King Herod, Magi from the east came to Jerusalem and asked, "Where is the one who has been born king of the Jews? We saw his star when it rose and have come to worship him." (Matt 2:1–2)*

There has been a great deal of controversy over the centuries about what this 'Star of Bethlehem' might really have been. Was it a comet? An alignment of planets in the night sky? A supernatural sign? We may not know the physical origins of this star, but there is no doubt as to its symbolic significance.

I love to watch the stars at night. They attract my attention in a way I cannot ignore, as they convey to me a sense of greatness, eternity, and vast unending space. They also speak to me of the glory of God the creator; and for me it makes sense that the creator of the stars must be greater and more powerful, a much brighter 'star' than any other.

Before the birth of Jesus, a child was born to the priest Zechariah and his wife Elizabeth who would become known as John the Baptist. The angel Gabriel had told Zechariah of the unique role of his son—that he would introduce the Messiah, Jesus, to his people Israel, that they might receive the forgiveness of sins. When John was born, Zechariah praised God and prophesied about his son's ministry. He said:

> *And you, my child, will be called a prophet of the Most High; for you will go on before the Lord to prepare the way for him, to give his people the knowledge of salvation through the forgiveness of their sins (Luke 2:76–77)*

Then he said of Jesus:

> *because of the tender mercy of our God, by which the rising sun will come to us from heaven (Luke 1:78)*

By comparing the coming of Jesus with the sunrise, Zechariah reveals why Jesus is called 'the bright morning star'. Although the sun is the nearest star to earth, the creator of the sun has come even nearer, appearing on earth in the person of Jesus. Jesus is a sunrise from heaven itself; he is the one of whom Charles Wesley wrote: 'light and life to all he brings—risen with healing in his wings!'

As he lives and reigns from his heavenly throne, Jesus—who made the stars—remains the centre of attraction in heaven, and for his people on earth, brighter than any star:

> *"I, Jesus, have sent my angel to testify to you about these things for the churches. I am the root and the descendant of David, the bright morning star!" (Rev 22:16)*

It was not the star above Bethlehem that we should focus on, but the 'star' who lay in Bethlehem, whom the wise men sought. This star was the light who brought forgiveness of sin for them—and for us.

Glass Baubles

Are you hanging symbols of God's love on your Christmas tree?

The coloured balls or baubles are essentially globes, and represent the beautiful world which God has created, and which he loves. When I say that God loves the world, I don't just mean that God cares for every plant and animal he has created, but that God has a special love for every single man, woman, boy and girl in the whole world.

> For God so loved the world that he gave his only Son, so that everyone who believes in him may not perish but may have eternal life. (John 3:16)

God's love for all people is so great it can only be measured in terms of the size and cost of the gift it was willing to give.

Imagine the whole world being held as a prisoner by a wicked terrorist, an enemy of God, who locked it in a cage formed from humanity's sin and rebellion. The original beauty of earth was spoiled, and violence and hate became the dominant forces in people's lives. What price could be paid so that the cage might be opened and we—together with the rest of creation—might be set free?

The ransom price was great drops of sweat, and bitter tears which flowed from Jesus' eyes in the garden of Gethsemane; it was thick drops of blood shed when he hung on the cross. These were not the tears and blood of any mere man, but of the eternal Son of God who became flesh at Christmas that by his death he might redeem us from Satan's power.

Even if I were to put solid silver or gold baubles on my Christmas tree, the price Jesus was willing to pay to ransom creation cost more:

It was not with perishable things such as silver or gold that you were redeemed from the empty way of life handed down to you from your ancestors, but with the precious blood of Christ, a lamb without blemish or defect. (1 Peter 1:18–19)

Being 'redeemed' means that we now belong to God, having been 'bought with a price'. Because of what Jesus did on the cross, not only will all believers one day be set free from the damaging effects of sin, but so will the whole of creation:

> the creation itself will be liberated from its bondage to decay and brought into the freedom and glory of the children of God. (Rom 8:21)

So this year, when you place a bauble on your Christmas tree, take it as the pledge that one day, the glory and beauty of creation will be fully restored, and that God's people will dwell with him forever in a new heaven and a new earth.

> Then I saw "a new heaven and a new earth," for the first heaven and the first earth had passed away, and there was no longer any sea. (Rev 21:1)

The Lights

The lights I put on the Christmas tree remind me that Jesus said:

"I am the light of the world. Whoever follows me will never walk in darkness but will have the light of life." John 8:12

Jesus came to bring us from the darkness of sin to the light of friendship with God.

I once saw a beautiful painting by the Dutch artist Gerard van Honthorst (c. 1622) titled 'The Adoration of the Shepherds'. The original painting is housed in the Wallraf-Richartz Museum in Cologne, Germany. The scene depicts Mary and Joseph with Jesus, who is lying in a manger in a darkened stable. Even though the night is dark, there is light—it is coming from the manger, shining out from the new-born Jesus who is the light of the world.

Light is a universal symbol of hope, and all over the world candles are often lit as a sign of hope and triumph over tragic circumstances. The birth of the Christ child brings hope to the world as it faces the darkness and despair of death and separation from God. God is light, and Christ lights the path that reunites us with him, so that we can walk in the light in renewed fellowship with God. As a result, we no longer need be estranged from him by our sin, but we can be reconciled, reunited, and forgiven.

This hope remains certain, because there will never be a time when the child of God will be separated from him:

For I am convinced that neither death nor life, neither angels nor demons, neither the present nor the future, nor any powers, neither height nor depth, nor anything else in all creation, will be able to separate us from the love of God that is in Christ Jesus our Lord. (Rom 8:38–39)

Our hope goes beyond this life, into the next. The Bible says that Jesus Christ is our hope, and that:

We have this hope as an anchor for the soul, firm and secure. It enters the inner sanctuary behind the curtain, where our forerunner, Jesus, has entered on our behalf. He has become a high priest forever, in the order of Melchizedek. (Heb 6:19–20)

Since Jesus Christ lives forever, continually representing us as our high priest before God, death can no longer hold any terrors for the Christian. When the time comes for us to finally leave this world, it will not be into the dark unknown, but into the light and joy of God our Father's home in heaven:

The sun will no more be your light by day, nor will the brightness of the moon shine on you, for the Lord will be your everlasting light, and your God will be your glory. Your sun will never set again, and your moon will wane no more; the Lord will be your everlasting light, and your days of sorrow will end. (Isaiah 60:19–20)

The Crown of Tinsel

A crown of golden tinsel finishes the decoration of my Christmas tree.

The tinsel reminds me of the glittering crown which Jesus now wears as he sits on a throne at God's right hand as Lord of heaven and earth. The apostle John caught a glimpse of this crown as he received his vision of heaven:

> *I looked, and there before me was a white cloud, and seated on the cloud was one like a son of man with a crown of gold on his head. (Rev 14:14)*

John went on to say that Jesus was wearing many crowns, a sign of his position as absolute Lord of all things.

> *His eyes are like blazing fire, and on his head are many crowns. (Rev 19:12)*

But once, my King Jesus wore a different crown on the cross, where he died to take away my sin, he wore a crown of painful thorns. Wicked men platted these sharp thorns into a crown and placed it roughly on Jesus' head as they ridiculed and mocked him.

However, after Jesus died on the cross, he rose again from the dead, and now he is alive in heaven where he wears a beautiful crown of glory which will last forever and ever!

Jesus is the King of kings and the Lord of lords. When you put your faith in him, you will have eternal life and become a child of God. Then if you serve the Lord Jesus every day, one day he will give you a beautiful crown of glory.

> *Now there is in store for me the crown of righteousness, which the Lord, the righteous Judge, will award to me on that day—and not only to me, but also to all who have longed for his appearing. (2 Tim 4:8)*

Just as the wise men laid their gifts of gold, frankincense, and myrrh at the feet of the infant Jesus, so God's people surround his throne in heaven and place their crowns, at his feet. The Bible pictures them casting their crowns before him, meaning that we will gladly give back to God everything we have:

> *The twenty-four elders throw themselves to the ground before the one who sits on the throne and worship the one who lives forever and ever, and they offer their crowns before his throne, saying: "You are worthy, our Lord and God, to receive glory and honor and power, since you created all things, and because of your will they existed and were created!" (Rev 4:10–11)*

Are you giving everything you have for God—the love of all your heart and soul? Are you giving the best of your time and energy to his service? If not, why not? Christmas is just the time to remember that King Jesus really is worthy of all our praise and worship.

The Gifts

On my Christmas tree, I hang little gifts, wrapped, and tied with coloured ribbons, plus candy canes and foil-covered chocolates for the children.

Every year, we arrange the bigger presents from friends and family beneath the Christmas tree to be opened on the big day! Look at the children shaking them and trying to guess what's inside!

The giving of gifts at Christmas may have begun in memory of the wise men who brought precious gifts to Jesus: gold, frankincense, and myrrh.

But the greatest gift of all is the gift which God gave for the world, the gift of his only Son. God's gift is amazing because when we unwrap it we find many gifts inside. Love, joy, peace, blessing and the hope of eternal life are all wrapped up in one tiny infant package—Jesus!

Do you know that eternal life is a gift from God? We cannot buy it neither can we earn it by our good deeds. God freely gives us the gift of eternal life when we trust His Son Jesus who died and rose again for us.

But there is a gift I can give to Jesus this Christmas. I can respond to his offer of eternal life with love and faith. What can I give to Jesus this Christmas? ... I can give him my heart!

Then when I get to heaven, I can join all of God's people who surround his throne to place their gifts at his feet. After all, everything that we have belongs to God, even our lives are his precious gift—and so we can only give back to God what he has first given to us:

> Who has ever given to God, that God should repay them?" For from him and through him and for him are all things. To him be the glory forever! Amen. (Rom 11:35–36)

Even so, in heaven God will have plenty more gifts to give to those who have served him on earth:

> "Listen!" says Jesus. "I am coming soon! I will bring my rewards with me, to give to each one according to what he has done. (Rev 22:12 GNB)

I'm too old now to wait for Father Christmas to come down the chimney with his sack of toys! However, I am waiting for the eternal gifts which God has promised to all who believe; eternal peace and everlasting joy in heaven.

> He will wipe away every tear from their eyes, and death will not exist any more -- or mourning, or crying, or pain, for the former things have ceased to exist." (Rev 21:4)

Until then, may I wish you a Christ-filled Christmas—a Christmas full of peace and happiness, with the promise of more to come!

Merry Christmas

By comparing the coming of Jesus with the sunrise, Zechariah reveals why Jesus is called 'the bright morning star'. Although the sun is the nearest star to earth, the creator of the sun has come even nearer, appearing on earth in the person of Jesus. Jesus is a sunrise from heaven itself; he is the one of whom Charles Wesley wrote: 'light and life to all he brings—risen with healing in his wings!'

As he lives and reigns from his heavenly throne, Jesus—who made the stars—remains the centre of attraction in heaven, and for his people on earth, brighter than any star:

> *"I, Jesus, have sent my angel to testify to you about these things for the churches. I am the root and the descendant of David, the bright morning star!" (Rev 22:16)*

It was not the star above Bethlehem that we should focus on, but the 'star' who lay in Bethlehem, whom the wise men sought. This star was the light who brought forgiveness of sin for them—and for us.